Ravin' About

Adult coloring book. Spend some time and color the smartest bird in raven designs. Detailed and simple birds that you can color.

Note From The Author: **Reviews are gold to authors! If you've enjoyed this book, would you please consider rating and reviewing it?**

DETAILED AND SIMPLE DESIGNS

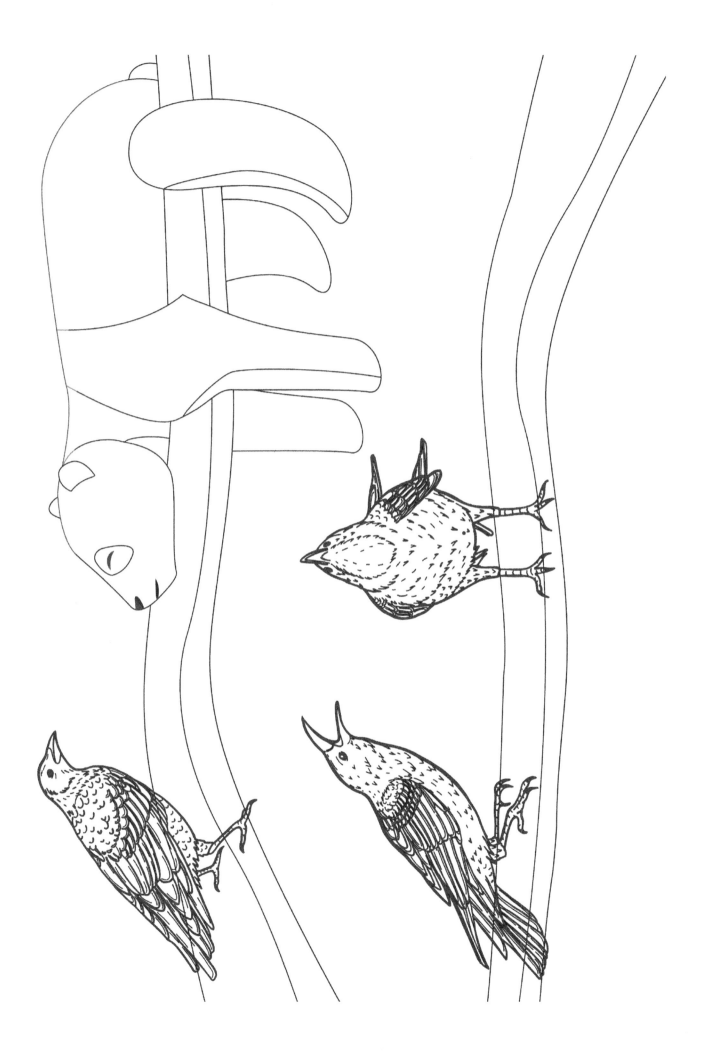

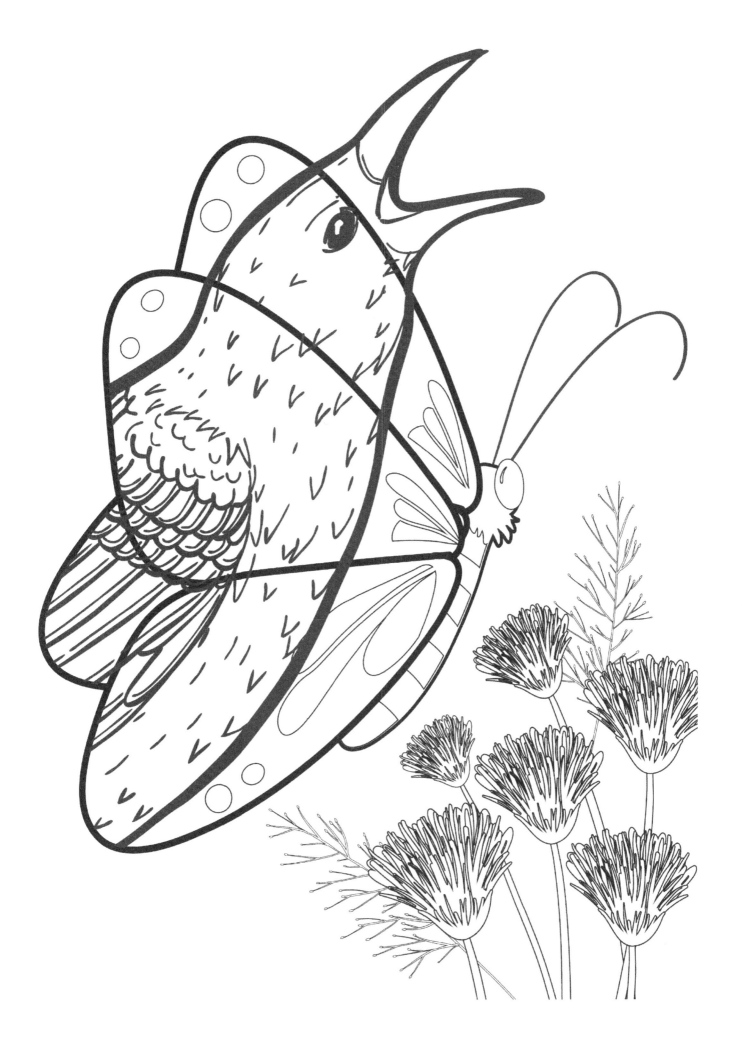

ACKNOWLEDGEMENTS

Appreciation goes out to those who contributed inspiration and support for my coloring books. Thanks to Rebecca Miller, Lea Johnson and Dale Franks. Everyone who has supported this edition extends their hope that readers have found it to be fun and entertaining.

AFTERWORD

If you have any thoughts, suggestions or tips for my next coloring book, please contact the author. Your feedback is welcome.

Reviews are gold to authors! If you've enjoyed this book, would you please consider commenting or rating it? Any feedback will help me improve future coloring book titles.

Made in the USA
Las Vegas, NV
24 May 2024

90329579R00033